The Perfect Love Connection

Carol Randell

AB **ASPECT Books**
www.ASPECTBooks.com

Copyright © 2014 Carol Randell
Copyright © 2014 Aspect Books
ISBN-13: 978-1-4796-0370-1 (Paperback)
ISBN-13: 978-1-4796-0371-8 (ePub)
ISBN-13: 978-1-4796-0372-5 (Mobi)

All scripture quotations, unless otherwise indicated, are taken from the King James Version. Public domain.

Scripture quotations marked NIV are taken from the Holy Bible, New International Version®, NIV®. Copyright © 1973, 1978, 1984, 2011 by Biblica, Inc.™ Used by permission of Zondervan. All rights reserved worldwide.

Published by

AB ASPECT Books
www.ASPECTBooks.com

Introduction

I often wonder why we go through so many trials. What is the meaning of life and the purpose for our existence? In the midst of these questions and struggles, I remember that God has a purpose for each of us, and I believe that until we walk within that purpose we are void of happiness and fulfillment.

There are many like me who don't understand the challenges of this life. But how can you or I, one solitary life, make a difference in the lives of others? In order to impact someone else's life, we must share our experience of how God has made a difference in our life. Life with Jesus is joyful, despite the sorrows that exist in this sinful world.

In days of old people often named their children based on what character trait they wanted them to have. There were meanings attached with each name. In the Bible, God changed the names of individuals such as Jacob and Abram because He wanted to give them a new meaning in life. Jeremiah 29:11 says, "For I know the thoughts that I think toward you, saith the Lord, thoughts of peace, and not of evil, to give you an expected end."

Despite whatever name given to an individual by their parents, God has a name for each of His children that showcases the greatness He has in store for them. God has plans to prosper us! We often look at prosperity in terms of our current financial situation, but prosperity can mean life, health, strength, or just a deeper relationship with God. Everything on this earth is temporary, but a relationship with Christ is eternal.

As I think about the name my parents gave me, I wonder if it matches the name God has picked out for me. My name, Carol, is supposed to mean song of joy, and although I enjoy music, especially Christmas carols that speak of God's great gift to the world, my life has been anything but joyful. Life has been very disappointing for me. Dreams have not come true, and I have experienced pain, hurt, and heartache.

My first hurt began as a child growing up with an alcoholic father. He was functional during the week, but Friday was his party night. Once I reached adulthood, I stumbled through two bad marriages. Based on my childhood, I was not equipped to make a wise decision about finding the right husband. I was taken advantage of in my first marriage, but I was too naïve to see it, and my second marriage was a repeat of what I grew up with.

Now, bruised and battered by life, I am looking to God and asking, what is my name? Is it really Carol, meaning song of joy? Or do You have something else in mind? I long for the day when I will experience the promise that John wrote about in Revelation 2:17, "He that hath an ear, let him hear what the Spirit saith unto the churches; to him that overcometh will I give … a white stone, and in the stone a new name written, which no man knoweth saving he that receiveth it."

We serve an intimate God who wants a relationship with us! However, if we don't take the time to kindle this intimate relationship here on earth, we will not know the King when He returns, and we will miss out on spending eternity with Him. It is my goal that despite the disappointments here on earth to one day experience the joy of heaven and meet my Bridegroom.

"Been there. Done that. Got the t-shirt!" Have you heard this saying? I say it a lot, but the truth is that most of the time when I get the T-shirt, I want to return it. "T-shirt experiences" can leave lasting painful memories, but God can wipe away every tear. Although pain and suffering are a part of living on this earth, God has promised to restore everything in the new earth.

Beyond Disappointment

The following psalm depicts the misery of life and the joy of trusting in God: "They cried unto thee, and were delivered: they trusted in thee, and were not confounded. But I am a worm, and no man; a reproach of men, and despised of the people. All they that see me laugh me to scorn: they shoot out the lip, they shake the head, saying, he trusted on the Lord that he would deliver him: let him deliver him, seeing he delighted in him. But thou art he that took me out of the womb: thou didst make me hope when I was upon my mother's breasts. I was cast upon thee from the womb: thou art my God from my mother's belly. Be not far from me; for trouble is near; for there is none to help" (Ps. 22:5–11).

Disappointment often occurs when our desires, hopes, or expectations are unfulfilled. When I was younger, people told me repeatedly that I was born on a bad date. *What's wrong with October 22?* I thought. As I grew older, I learned about the Great Disappointment that occurred on October 22, 1844, when many Advent believers thought Christ would return and take them to heaven. In the days and weeks after October 22, some of the believers lost faith and gave up on God, while others diligently searched the Scriptures for truth.

I can imagine how those people must have felt. I, too, have expected and anticipated something good at times only to find that things didn't work out as I had hoped they would. I have experienced disappointments in my life, and I want to share some of my thoughts and life lessons as related to relationships.

Relationships are the most valuable asset we have here on earth. Family is valuable and important. However, relationships sometimes fall apart no matter how hard we work to keep them together. In order to succeed, God must be the center of the home. The challenge is when your faith grows weak because of so many failed relationships, which is what began to happen in my life. I lacked understanding of what a true relationship looked like. I wanted to be loved by my earthly father, but because of the hurt I experienced from my father, I began to doubt my relationship with my heavenly Father, and I felt that He didn't care either.

"God," I cried out, "can't You see the tears and hear my pleas as my husband continues to drink and upset our home. This is definitely not what I want for my life; I don't want it to be a repeat of what I grew up with. Have mercy on me, Lord, for I did not let You take the lead in my choice of a marriage partner, and my life is a mess."

I began to realize that anything outside of God's plan is unfulfilling and dark. It may seem like fun for a while, but when we come to our senses, we realize what an awful mess we are in that only God is qualified to deal with. "Oh ye of little faith," Jesus often told His disciples. I am afraid I fall into this same condition. I lack faith and trust in God over certain areas of my life. And because of this, I have experienced some severe consequences in which divine intervention has been called upon to heal. Even as I write this I still feel the hand of God healing me in areas of my life that only He can reach. So be encouraged. You may have wounds from current or past relationships that you feel will never heal, but God can heal you and make you whole.

Roman 8:28 is a wonderful promise to hold on to when faced with the challenges of life: "And we know that all things work together for good to them that love God, to them who are the called according to his purpose." We must also remember that the Bible says, "I can do all things through Christ which strengtheneth me" (Phil. 4:13). If we submit to God and allow Him to make some necessary changes in our lives, maybe our outlook won't be so disappointing. And even if our current circumstances may appear disappointing, you can rest assured that if you love God He is working it out for your good.

Finding a Good Man

During my childhood God spoke to me through dreams and showed me some dark places in my life where sin had taken hold of me. I thought I was a pretty good person, but He began to call me to Himself and show me how I would turn out if I did not choose Him. I had multiple dreams about the judgment day, and every time I was lost. In these dreams I heard God speaking, telling me, that this would be my destiny without Him. You see, many of us grow up believing that if we are good we will be rewarded. Although as humans it is nice to reward good behavior, God reminds us that all our righteousness is as filthy rags.

Thinking about these dreams prompted me, at the young age of fourteen, to surrender my heart to God. It was the very best decision I made. Although I didn't realize that I needed to totally surrender to God and let Him be the leader of my life. I accepted salvation, but I had problems giving Him complete control.

Even today, after serving God for thirty-six years, it is an area I still need to improve. Through all my good and bad choices, God has been faithful. I ask myself why I haven't gotten kicked to the curb yet, but then I remember that God is not like humans. People say that "a good man is hard to find." But I disagree because God has proven to be that good Man! I am so thankful to have a good Man in my life who loves me unconditionally; looks on the inside, not the outside; and is patient, kind, longsuffering, gentle, and merciful. Who doesn't want a man like that?

Still Looking

There is an old saying about looking for love in all the wrong places. As I thought about what that meant, I came up with some wrong places to find a man. One is in a club, especially if you are a Christian. When making decisions, God asks us to use our brain and apply the principles in His Word. If you are looking for someone with Christian values, then you need to go to places where you can meet other Christians.

Of course, what makes us think we have to go looking in the first place? Did Adam wander around the garden looking for Eve? No. He talked with God, and when he realized his need of a companion, God provided for that need. Therein lies the solution: seek God first, and all the other things we need will be given to us.

It's hard to find a good man or woman these days, especially when I consider the word good from a biblical perspective: "There is none good but one, that is, God" (Mark 10:18). So since there are no good men or women, what is the point of looking? I encourage anyone looking for a spouse to look to God. He is good, and He will direct you to the person who is also looking for Him and who will be compatible with you.

Have you ever gone grocery shopping when you are hungry? What do you choose to buy? Everything! Because everything looks good when you are hungry. Just this week I went shopping when I was hungry, and I bought cookies, candy, and other snacks with little nutritional value. Yes, all of it tasted good, but none of it was good for me!

Only God in His wisdom knows who is the best person to be your spouse and to help you reach your long-term goal of heaven. Eternity is at stake, and a godly or ungodly spouse can make the difference in helping you to stay focused on Christ or pulling you away and leading you down a path of destruction. Your choices on this earth will dictate where you spend eternity.

It has been my experience that human flesh cannot be trusted. I have depended on myself to make decisions, and things have turned out horrible. We have to die daily to ourselves and allow the Spirit of God to live in us and guide us. Pray, fast, and pray and fast some more. Satan wants to destroy the family. He wants to destroy the values that are passed down from generation to generation in loving homes.

In addition to asking God to guide you to the right person, take time to get to know the person. See if his or her characteristics match that of Christ. Spend quality time talking together to see if you are compatible with one another. After all, marriage is a lifetime commitment.

Although you should look at the qualities of the other person, ultimately trust God to make the final selection. Trust God and look to Him for guidance. If you seek to follow God's will for your life, God will select someone whose purpose is to glorify Him.

It is God's desire that we are happy and that we follow His will, because He has our best interest in mind. In fact, the Bible says, "He maketh his sun to rise on the evil and on the good, and sendeth rain on the just and on the unjust" (Matt. 5:45). Sadly, so often we blame God for our disappointments, even though we have chosen not to listen to Him. We must also remember that we are living in a sinful world and that bad things will happen to good people. There is a philosophy that if we follow Christ nothing bad will happen to us. However, as long as we live here on this sinful planet, life will be full of problems.

Many state that God will give us the desires of our heart, but if our desires do not match His heavenly desires and His will for our life, then we have missed the boat. Our goal as Christians should be to develop a deeper relationship with God in preparation for spending eternity with Him in heaven. We must remember that God has our best interest in mind. God sees the outcome of our desires, and He tries to nudge us in a direction that will be best for us. We need to learn to trust God and give Him the final say on our decisions. If we follow this plan, we will be at peace even in the midst of our storms.

Dreams of Eternal Happiness

I love what Paul wrote to the Romans about the Jews and the law. The clarity of his works and his assurance of God's love is powerful.

> Now you, if you call yourself a Jew; if you rely
> on the law and boast in God; if you know his will
> and approve of what is superior because you are

instructed by the law; if you are convinced that you are a guide for the blind, a light for those who are in the dark, an instructor of the foolish, a teacher of little children, because you have in the law the embodiment of knowledge and truth—you, then, who teach others, do you not teach yourself? You who preach against stealing, do you steal? You who say that people should not commit adultery, do you commit adultery? You who abhor idols, do you rob temples? You who boast in the law, do you dishonor God by breaking the law? As it is written: 'God's name is blasphemed among the Gentiles because of you.' Circumcision has value if you observe the law, but if you break the law, you have become as though you had not been circumcised. So then, if those who are not circumcised keep the law's requirements, will they not be regarded as though they were circumcised? The one who is not circumcised physically and yet obeys the law will condemn you who, even though you have the written code and circumcision, are a law breaker. A person is not a Jew who is one only outwardly, nor is circumcision merely outward and physical. (Rom. 2:17–28, NIV)

Much of the book of Romans deals with salvation by faith and the assurance that the Gentiles were just as worthy to enter the kingdom of heaven as the Jews who were of the lineage of Abraham and had accepted Jesus as their Savior.

As I mentioned previously, God has always spoken to me in dreams. I remember God using dreams to draw me to Him as a child. The dreams I had about the judgment troubled me, for in my dream I was never ready for the judgment. Fortunately, the book of Romans gives me assurance of salvation through faith in Christ, regardless of the mistakes I have made on this earth.

I don't want to miss out on the joys and splendor of heaven. The Bible says, "Eye hath not seen, nor ear heard … the things which God hath prepared for them that love him" (1 Cor. 2:9). Every day I must take the time to ask God to teach me to love Him more. My relationship with Him is of infinite value to me, and when my relationship with God is strong, my relationships with others flourish. I appreciate and thank God for the dreams He has given me throughout the years—dreams that have refocused my mind on the most important goal, which is heaven.

Stolen Birthright

Outside of God, there is no joy! However, Satan constantly dangles things in front of us to entice us and try to draw us away from God. Of course, he only dangles that which he knows we will be tempted by. He's not going to dangle cheesecake in front of you if we don't like cheesecake. He's not going to bring you vanilla when your favorite flavor is chocolate.

In the story of Jacob and Esau, Satan tempted Jacob and Rebekah to take matters into their own hands regarding the birthright and not wait on God. Esau had sold his birthright to Jacob for some lentils and bread because Esau was dying of hunger and was focused on the present and not the future. But when it came time for Isaac to issue the birthright, Jacob and Rebekah failed to put their trust in God to fulfill what He had promised to Jacob before his birth, which was that he, the younger brother, would rule over his elder brother. Jacob's lack of trust in God's plan led to heartache and misery.

If God has promised you something, wait on Him to fulfill the promise. If you have asked God to help you find the right spouse, then wait on Him to bring someone into your life. If you have found the right person, wait on God for the right time to get married and keep yourself pure before your wedding. Many feel that if you are in a committed relationship anything goes. However, God wants us to save the sacred act of sex for marriage. If you are in a difficult relationship, seek God's will regarding how you should deal with your spouse. Divorce was never God's plan for married couples.

Many lives have been wrecked because of not listening to God's clear, simple instructions. Hearts have been broken, families destroyed, and diseases acquired because people go their own way and do their own thing is pursuit of temporary happiness. May we experience lasting joy by following God's plan for our lives.

The Desire of the Heart!

I love the promise of hope that is found in 2 Chronicles 7:14: "If my people, which are called by my name, shall humble themselves, and pray, and seek my face, and turn from their wicked ways; then will I hear from heaven, and will forgive their sin, and will heal their land." This promise reminds us that we are never too far from God that we can't turn around, ask for forgiveness, and start out fresh.

Solomon, the wisest man who ever lived, knew this well, for he wandered away from God and came back. Solomon had everything his heart desired. He had money, women, power, fame, and much more, yet he realized that without God his life was nothing. God is the only one who can fill that empty spot in our hearts. He is the only one who can satisfy our deepest longings.

Some of us get really angry with God when He does not answer our prayers as we expect. We get so frustrated when God does not give us this or that or when He does not allow us to have what we feel is the desire of our heart. Some people, like myself, even begin to challenge Him with His word: "Lord, You said in the Bible that You would give me the desires of my heart. And then when I tell you my desire, You don't give it to me. What's up with that, God? Why are You withholding that which is for my good or that which I desire?"

But remember, the flesh will get you in trouble because you cannot distinguish what is best. God says He is more willing to give us good gifts than our earthly parents. And most importantly, He wants to give us the gift of the Holy Ghost. The Comforter is your helper and friend; He will lead you in the right path. It will not be the most traveled or popular path, but it is the path that leads to eternal life. The empty spot in your heart is meant to be filled by God; He is the only one who can satisfy your desires.

Jeremiah 29:11–13 reminds us to turn our plans over to God: "For I know the thoughts that I think toward you, saith the LORD, thoughts of peace, and not of evil, to give you an expected end. Then shall ye call upon me, and ye shall go and pray unto me, and I will hearken unto you. And ye shall seek me, and find me, when ye shall search for me with all your heart."

Many time I thought I knew what was best for me, but I veered off the narrow path in pursuit of temporary happiness. However, I conclude, as Solomon, that all is vanity. My desires lead to unhappiness, heart break, and disappointment. If your desires do not line up with the Lord's plan for your life, step back and reevaluate your life. Ask God to help you trust in Him. He is the Pearl of Great Price, the treasure that cannot be brought. He is the one who can fulfill the desires of your heart.

The Man!

I marvel at Jesus's power and the love He showed to all human beings while on this earth. The story of Him healing the demoniac is one such story, and the response of the man says it all: "As Jesus was getting into the boat, the man who had been demon-possessed begged to go with him. Jesus did not let him, but said, 'Go home to your people and tell them how much the Lord has done for you, and how he has had mercy on you.' So the man went away and began to tell in the Decapolis how much Jesus had done for him. And all the people were amazed" (Mark 5:18–20, NIV).

If Jesus took time to heal a demon-possessed man, then there is hope for us. Life is full of disappointments and challenges, but when we don't allow God to have full control over our decisions, our troubles multiply and become unbearable. There is a saying that states, "Follow your heart," but I suggest not to follow your heart but to follow God. Our hearts are desperately wicked, like the Bible says, which I have personally found to be true.

In looking for a godly spouse, seek guidance from the Man who knows everything! God knows what is best, and He knows you better than you know yourself. He knows who will help you prepare for heaven and who would be a stumbling block. It is so easy to go against God and do things our way, but I urge you to listen to His voice and wait patiently until He brings the right person into your life.

When I get to heaven, I want to ask Mary Magdalene why she didn't bother with men after her conversion. According to the account we have in the Bible, she didn't marry after Jesus told her to go and sin no more.

It is my opinion that she stayed single because she had finally met the sweetest Man she had ever known, and no one could measure up to Jesus. Jesus showed her unconditional, genuine love when other men had used her and deceived her. Jesus treated her differently.

No one can compare to Jesus, for there is none like Him. There is no one else who has gone to such great lengths to prove His love for us. Jesus didn't just talk about love; He put His love into action. He hung on the cross to save everyone, even those who mistreated Him. After getting to know Someone like this who was willing to take our place and die for our sins, I pray that you will let Jesus have control. He only wants the very best for you. You don't have to continue wallowing in your disappointing life. Jesus is the solution. He is the Man!

None of the plans for my life have come to fruition in the area of relationships. I have failed God again and again with my lack of faith and trust in His divine plan, which is why I appreciate the grace that God has extended to me. This grace has led me to a new goal. I want to share His goodness with others, so they can also appreciate the gift of grace and salvation that He offers. Be encouraged. Our God is gracious and kind, not willing that anyone should perish. This is why I believe He is extending the doors of mercy longer. He wants everyone to choose Him. Yet He doesn't force His will on us. It is our choice whether we follow Him or not. He did not create us to be robots. He has given us free will to choose the direction we want to go. However, He stands at the door and knocks, readily waiting for us to open the door and welcome Him in.

Our choices determine where we will spend eternity. I encourage you; no, I beg you to choose God. Let Him guide you through this life and pick your mate. And the beauty of this plan is that when you learn to trust God in one area of your life, you will trust Him in other areas. All of this will prepare you for heaven and eternity with Christ.

> And I John saw the holy city, new Jerusalem, coming down from God out of heaven, prepared as a bride adorned for her husband. And I heard a great voice out of heaven saying, Behold, the tabernacle of God is with men, and he will dwell with them, and they shall be his people, and God himself shall be with them, and be their God. And God shall wipe away all tears from their eyes; and there shall be no more death, neither sorrow, nor crying, neither shall there be any more pain: for the former things are passed away. (Rev. 21:2–4)

When you hold on to God's hand, the blessings will follow. Even if the blessings are not realized on this earth, they are sure to follow in heaven where we will spend eternity with our perfect "spouse," our Savior.

We invite you to view the complete
selection of titles we publish at:

www.TEACHServices.com

Please write or e-mail us your praises, reactions, or
thoughts about this or any other book we publish at:

TEACH Services, Inc.
P U B L I S H I N G
www.TEACHServices.com ● (800) 367-1844

P.O. Box 954
Ringgold, GA 30736

info@TEACHServices.com

TEACH Services, Inc., titles may be purchased in bulk for
educational, business, fund-raising, or sales promotional use.
For information, please e-mail:

BulkSales@TEACHServices.com

Finally, if you are interested in seeing
your own book in print, please contact us at

publishing@TEACHServices.com

We would be happy to review your manuscript for free.

www.ingramcontent.com/pod-product-compliance
Lightning Source LLC
LaVergne TN
LVHW050047090426
835511LV00033B/2900